Copyright © 2023 by Jonathan A. Sinclair (Author)

This book is protected by copyright law and is intended solely for personal use. Reproduction, distribution, or any other form of use requires the written permission of the author. The information presented in this book is for educational and entertainment purposes only, and while every effort has been made to ensure its accuracy and completeness, no guarantees are made. The author is not providing legal, financial, medical, or professional advice, and readers should consult with a licensed professional before implementing any of the techniques discussed in this book. The content in this book has been sourced from various reliable sources, but readers should exercise their own judgment when using this information. The author is not responsible for any losses, direct or indirect, that may occur from the use of this book, including but not limited to errors, omissions, or inaccuracies.

We hope this book has been informative and helpful on your journey to understanding and celebrating older adults. Thank you for your interest and support!

Title: Triumphs of the Treble: Legendary European Football Clubs - Volume 2

Subtitle: Champions on Three Fronts

Series: Triumphs of the Treble: Legendary European Football Clubs

By Jonathan A. Sinclair

Celebrating Manchester City's Treble Triumph in the 2022-2023 Season!

The 2022-2023 season is remembered as a remarkable year for Manchester City Football Club. Their dominance and skill were on full display as they achieved the extraordinary feat of winning the treble. Led by their esteemed manager and a talented squad, Manchester City showcased exceptional form in the domestic league, securing the top spot and earning the coveted domestic league title. They also displayed their prowess in domestic cup competitions, triumphing in the FA Cup and adding another prestigious trophy to their collection.

However, the crowning jewel of their historic season came in the form of their UEFA Champions League triumph. In a tense and thrilling final against Inter Milan, Manchester City emerged victorious with a narrow 1-0 win. Facing one of Europe's most formidable teams, they exhibited resilience, skill, and mettle on the grandest stage, etching their name in football history and securing the most prestigious club trophy in European football. This treble-winning season solidifies their status as a football powerhouse and sets a new benchmark for excellence and ambition.

Manchester City's remarkable achievement, including their victory against Inter Milan in the UEFA Champions League final, will forever be etched in the memories of fans and football enthusiasts worldwide. It serves as a glorious chapter in the club's illustrious history, inspiring future generations and reminding us of the remarkable heights that can be attained through determination, skill, and a shared passion for the beautiful game.

Pep Guardiola: The Only Manager to Achieve the Treble with Multiple Clubs

In the world of European football, Pep Guardiola stands alone as the only manager to achieve the treble with multiple clubs. His first triumph came in the 2008-2009 season with FC Barcelona, where his tactical brilliance led them to secure the domestic league, domestic cup, and the UEFA Champions League. Now, at Manchester City in the hypothetical 2022-2023 season, Guardiola's managerial genius once again prevails as his team conquers the domestic league, domestic cup, and reaches the pinnacle of European football. Guardiola's unparalleled legacy and his ability to inspire future generations make him a true maestro of the game. His distinction will forever be etched in football history as a testament to innovation, dedication, and a profound understanding of the beautiful game.

Table of Contents

Introduction 8
   The significance of treble-winning seasons in European football 8
   Brief overview of Ajax Amsterdam, FC Barcelona, and Bayern Munich 12
   The anticipation and excitement surrounding the 1971-1972, 2008-2009, and 2019-2020 seasons 15

Chapter 1: Ajax Amsterdam - Season: 1971-1972 19
   The rise of Total Football and its influence on Ajax 19
   The domination of the Eredivisie 23
   The journey through the KNVB Cup 26
   The captivating run in the UEFA Champions League 30
   The final triumph and memorable performances 34

Chapter 2: FC Barcelona - Season: 2008-2009 38
   The era of Pep Guardiola and the transformation of Barcelona 38
   The battle for La Liga supremacy 42
   The pursuit of the Copa del Rey 46
   The mesmerizing UEFA Champions League campaign .. 50
   The iconic final and the triumph of style 54

Chapter 3: Bayern Munich - Season: 2019-2020 58
   Bayern Munich's dominance in German football 58
   The Bundesliga triumph 62

The DFB-Pokal journey 67
The UEFA Champions League run 71
The triumphant final and the treble glory 75

Chapter 4: Legends and Key Figures 78
Exploring the legendary figures associated with each club 78
The impact of iconic players, coaches, and key personnel 82
The memorable contributions and defining moments 86

Chapter 5: Legacy and Impact 92
The lasting legacy of the treble-winning seasons 92
The impact on the clubs, fans, and football landscape ... 96
The influence on subsequent generations and future aspirations 100

Conclusion 104
Reflecting on the significance of these treble-winning seasons 104
The enduring impact on the clubs' histories 108
The legacy of Ajax Amsterdam, FC Barcelona, and Bayern Munich 112

Key Terms and Definitions 117
Supporting Materials 120

Introduction

The significance of treble-winning seasons in European football

In the realm of European football, few achievements resonate as profoundly as winning the treble - the triumphant feat of securing three major trophies in a single season. This extraordinary accomplishment, achieved by only a handful of legendary clubs, embodies the pinnacle of success and represents a rare combination of talent, skill, determination, and sheer dominance.

Treble-winning seasons have left an indelible mark on the history of European football, captivating the imaginations of fans, pundits, and players alike. These remarkable campaigns transcend the boundaries of individual competitions, elevating clubs to legendary status and immortalizing their achievements in the annals of the sport. As we delve into the treble-winning seasons of Ajax Amsterdam, FC Barcelona, and Bayern Munich, we embark on a journey that unveils the extraordinary significance of these exceptional triumphs.

1. A Testament to Unrivaled Excellence

The treble-winning seasons stand as a testament to unrivaled excellence in European football. They demonstrate the remarkable ability of a club to navigate and conquer multiple competitions simultaneously, showcasing an unmatched level of consistency, skill, and tactical prowess. These triumphs signify the pinnacle of achievement, raising the bar for future generations of footballers and clubs.

2. The Pursuit of Domestic Supremacy

At the heart of the treble-winning seasons lies the conquest of domestic competitions. Securing the league title, often the most coveted prize in a country's football landscape, showcases a club's sustained dominance over an entire season. The quest for domestic supremacy demands unwavering commitment, mental fortitude, and the ability to overcome formidable opponents week after week.

3. The Glory of Cup Triumphs

In addition to league success, treble-winning seasons are marked by victorious cup campaigns. Competing in knockout tournaments such as the KNVB Cup, Copa del Rey, and the DFB-Pokal, clubs must navigate through treacherous fixtures, facing off against fellow giants and battling against the unpredictability of one-off matches. These cup competitions provide an avenue for clubs to showcase their depth, resilience, and ability to perform under pressure.

4. The European Crown Jewel: The UEFA Champions League

While domestic triumphs are a remarkable accomplishment in their own right, it is the conquest of the UEFA Champions League that elevates a treble-winning season to the realm of greatness. The Champions League represents the ultimate stage for European football, pitting the continent's elite against each other in a battle for supremacy. The grueling campaign, featuring home and away fixtures against the finest clubs, tests a team's mettle, strategy, and adaptability. Emerging victorious from this highly competitive tournament signifies a club's ability to conquer the best in Europe, etching their name in the history books and forging a legacy that endures.

5. Inspiration for Generations to Come

The significance of treble-winning seasons extends far beyond the immediate glory and adulation. These campaigns inspire generations of footballers, managers, and fans, setting the standard for excellence and providing a blueprint for success. The accomplishments of Ajax Amsterdam, FC Barcelona, and Bayern Munich continue to resonate, influencing the way the game is played, the tactics employed, and the aspirations of clubs around the world. Young players grow up dreaming of replicating the heroics of their idols, driven by the desire to etch their names alongside the legends of the past.

Conclusion

The significance of treble-winning seasons in European football cannot be overstated. These exceptional campaigns showcase the relentless pursuit of excellence, the triumph over domestic rivals, the glory of cup victories, and the ultimate conquest of the UEFA Champions League. They provide a source of inspiration for players and fans alike, shaping the landscape of the sport and leaving an indelible mark on the history of the clubs involved. As we delve into the treble-winning seasons of Ajax Amsterdam, FC Barcelona, and Bayern Munich, we embark on a journey that celebrates the extraordinary and recognizes the enduring impact of these iconic achievements.

Brief overview of Ajax Amsterdam, FC Barcelona, and Bayern Munich

In the realm of European football, certain clubs have etched their names into the annals of history through their remarkable achievements. Ajax Amsterdam, FC Barcelona, and Bayern Munich stand among the greatest and most successful clubs, not only in their respective countries but also on the continental stage. This brief overview will delve into the rich histories, traditions, and successes of these iconic clubs, providing insight into their significance in the footballing world.

1. Ajax Amsterdam: The Dutch Pioneers of Total Football

Ajax Amsterdam, founded in 1900, emerged as a powerhouse during the late 1960s and early 1970s under the visionary leadership of Rinus Michels and Johan Cruyff. The club revolutionized the game with their implementation of Total Football, a dynamic and fluid style of play that emphasized positional interchangeability and attacking creativity. With a focus on homegrown talent, Ajax dominated the Eredivisie, capturing numerous league titles during this period. Their rise culminated in the treble-winning season of 1971-1972, where they conquered the Dutch league, the KNVB Cup, and the prestigious UEFA

Champions League, leaving an indelible mark on the history of the beautiful game.

2. FC Barcelona: The Catalan Giants and the Era of Pep Guardiola

FC Barcelona, founded in 1899, has a storied history rooted in the Catalan identity and a commitment to attractive, possession-based football. In recent times, the club has reached unprecedented heights under the guidance of legendary coach Pep Guardiola. Guardiola's reign saw Barcelona redefine the parameters of success, as they secured multiple La Liga titles and established themselves as a dominant force in Spanish football. FC Barcelona's treble-winning season of 2008-2009 epitomized their style, as they combined skillful ball movement, intelligent positional play, and the genius of Lionel Messi to triumph in the domestic league, the Copa del Rey, and the UEFA Champions League.

3. Bayern Munich: German Powerhouse and the Modern Era

Bayern Munich, founded in 1900, represents the epitome of German football excellence. Known for their unrivaled domestic dominance and formidable European campaigns, Bayern Munich has forged a legacy built on a rich tradition of success. The club's treble-winning season of 2019-2020 showcased their relentless pursuit of silverware.

With an enviable blend of German efficiency and attacking prowess, Bayern Munich claimed the Bundesliga title, triumphed in the DFB-Pokal, and conquered Europe by winning the UEFA Champions League. Under the tutelage of coaches such as Jupp Heynckes and Hansi Flick, Bayern Munich has solidified its position as one of the most formidable clubs in European football.

Conclusion

Ajax Amsterdam, FC Barcelona, and Bayern Munich represent the crème de la crème of European football. With storied histories, distinctive footballing philosophies, and a tradition of success, these clubs have left an indelible mark on the sport. From Ajax's Total Football revolution to Barcelona's possession-based wizardry and Bayern Munich's German powerhouse dominance, their achievements have captivated fans and inspired future generations. As we delve deeper into their treble-winning seasons, we will witness the magic, resilience, and unparalleled brilliance that have propelled these clubs to the zenith of footballing greatness.

The anticipation and excitement surrounding the 1971-1972, 2008-2009, and 2019-2020 seasons

The treble-winning seasons of Ajax Amsterdam, FC Barcelona, and Bayern Munich in 1971-1972, 2008-2009, and 2019-2020 respectively, were characterized not only by their remarkable achievements but also by the anticipation and excitement that surrounded these historic campaigns. In this section, we delve into the context, narratives, and fervor that accompanied these iconic seasons, capturing the essence of the footballing world as it awaited the unfolding of history.

1. 1971-1972: Ajax Amsterdam's Total Football Revolution

The anticipation surrounding Ajax Amsterdam's treble-winning season of 1971-1972 was palpable as Rinus Michels' Total Football philosophy took hold. With Johan Cruyff as the embodiment of their attacking flair and positional interchangeability, Ajax captured the imagination of football fans across Europe. The anticipation grew as they dominated the Eredivisie with their mesmerizing brand of football, culminating in a scintillating UEFA Champions League campaign that showcased their technical brilliance and innovative tactics.

2. 2008-2009: FC Barcelona's Rise under Pep Guardiola

The 2008-2009 season was marked by the anticipation of FC Barcelona's resurgence under the guidance of Pep Guardiola. After a period of relative underachievement, the appointment of Guardiola as head coach sparked a renewed sense of optimism. The anticipation grew as Barcelona's mesmerizing brand of possession-based football, led by maestros such as Lionel Messi, Xavi Hernandez, and Andres Iniesta, unfolded. As they mounted a captivating challenge for La Liga supremacy and embarked on their UEFA Champions League journey, the excitement among fans reached a fever pitch.

3. 2019-2020: Bayern Munich's European Dominance

The 2019-2020 season brought heightened anticipation for Bayern Munich as they sought to reclaim their position among Europe's elite. With a blend of experienced stalwarts and emerging talents, including Robert Lewandowski, Thomas Muller, and Alphonso Davies, Bayern Munich entered the season with lofty aspirations. The anticipation centered around their dominance in the Bundesliga and their pursuit of continental glory in the UEFA Champions League. The excitement peaked as they produced scintillating performances, dismantling opponents with ruthless efficiency and captivating fans with their attacking prowess.

5. The Narrative Arcs and Subplots

Within the broader anticipation and excitement of these treble-winning seasons, there were numerous narrative arcs and subplots that heightened the drama and added to the allure of the campaigns. These included rivalries, individual storylines, historic milestones, and moments of redemption. The anticipation of intense encounters between giants of the game, the emergence of young talents, and the pursuit of records and legacies all contributed to the tapestry of excitement that surrounded these seasons.

6. The Global Footballing Community and Fan Perspectives

The anticipation and excitement surrounding these treble-winning seasons extended far beyond the clubs and their immediate supporters. Football fans from around the world eagerly followed the narratives, debates, and predictions surrounding these iconic campaigns. Through media coverage, fan forums, and social media, supporters engaged in passionate discussions, sharing their hopes, dreams, and predictions, further heightening the anticipation and fostering a sense of unity and shared excitement.

Conclusion

The anticipation and excitement surrounding treble-winning seasons in European football are unrivaled. The build-up, challenges faced, and unforgettable moments create an atmosphere of electric anticipation and unparalleled excitement. The treble-winning seasons of Ajax Amsterdam, FC Barcelona, and Bayern Munich captured the imaginations of fans around the world, cementing their place in footballing history. These seasons continue to serve as reminders of the exhilarating nature of the sport, where dreams are realized, underdogs triumph, and legendary clubs etch their names in the annals of European football.

Chapter 1: Ajax Amsterdam - Season: 1971-1972
The rise of Total Football and its influence on Ajax

The treble-winning season of 1971-1972 marked a watershed moment in the history of Ajax Amsterdam. At the heart of their success was the revolutionary footballing philosophy known as Total Football. In this chapter, we delve into the rise of Total Football and its profound influence on Ajax, exploring how this innovative approach to the game transformed the club's fortunes and left an enduring legacy in the world of football.

1. The Birth of Total Football: The Influence of Rinus Michels

The roots of Total Football can be traced back to Rinus Michels, a visionary coach who sought to create a system that prioritized fluidity, versatility, and collective understanding on the field. Michels, along with his coaching staff and a group of talented players, laid the foundations of a revolutionary style of play that would redefine football tactics. We examine Michels' coaching philosophy, his emphasis on positional interchangeability, and the tactical innovations that laid the groundwork for Total Football.

2. The Ajax Academy: The Crucible of Talent

Central to Ajax's success during the treble-winning season was the club's renowned youth academy, known for its emphasis on technical skills, tactical understanding, and nurturing young talents. We explore the Ajax Academy's role in the development of players such as Johan Cruyff, Johan Neeskens, and Ruud Krol, who became the torchbearers of Total Football. The chapter highlights the club's commitment to homegrown talent and its role in creating a cohesive and dynamic team.

3. Total Football in Action: The Principles and Execution

Total Football was characterized by specific principles that allowed Ajax to dominate their opponents with their fluidity and attacking prowess. We delve into the key tenets of Total Football, including positional interchangeability, pressing, off-the-ball movement, and collective responsibility. Through insightful analysis and memorable anecdotes, we explore how these principles were executed on the field, resulting in a breathtaking brand of football that captivated fans and revolutionized the game.

4. The Influence of Johan Cruyff: The Maestro of Total Football

No discussion of Total Football and Ajax's success is complete without recognizing the immense influence of Johan Cruyff. As the epitome of the Total Football philosophy, Cruyff's vision, technique, and footballing intelligence were instrumental in shaping Ajax's playing style. We delve into Cruyff's impact, both as a player and as a cultural icon, examining his ability to seamlessly adapt to various positions and his role as a catalyst for Ajax's success during the treble-winning season.

5. The Global Impact and Legacy of Total Football

The rise of Total Football and Ajax's triumphant season had a far-reaching impact on the global footballing landscape. We explore how Ajax's success reverberated across Europe, inspiring clubs and national teams to adopt the principles of Total Football. The chapter examines how clubs such as Barcelona, Bayern Munich, and the Dutch national team embraced elements of Total Football, showcasing its lasting influence on the modern game.

Conclusion

The rise of Total Football and its influence on Ajax Amsterdam during the 1971-1972 treble-winning season stands as a landmark moment in football history. Rinus Michels' visionary approach, combined with the talent nurtured in the Ajax Academy and the genius of Johan Cruyff, paved the way for a style of play that captivated the world. The principles of Total Football continue to shape football tactics, emphasizing fluidity, versatility, and collective brilliance. Ajax's success not only secured their place among the footballing elite but also left an indelible mark on the evolution of the beautiful game.

The domination of the Eredivisie

In the treble-winning season of 1971-1972, Ajax Amsterdam not only conquered Europe but also asserted their dominance in the domestic league, the Eredivisie. This chapter explores Ajax's relentless pursuit of success in the Eredivisie, examining their remarkable performances, their rivals, and the key factors that propelled them to unparalleled heights of achievement.

1. Ajax's Eredivisie Pedigree: Building a Foundation for Success

To understand Ajax's domination of the Eredivisie during the 1971-1972 season, we must first trace their path to success. We delve into the club's earlier triumphs, the development of their youth academy, and the key figures who laid the foundation for their future dominance. From their first league title to the emergence of Rinus Michels and the arrival of a generation of talented players, we unravel the story of Ajax's rise to prominence in Dutch football.

2. The 1970-1971 Season: A Glimpse of Things to Come

The Eredivisie campaign leading up to Ajax's treble-winning season provided a glimpse of their potential dominance. We analyze Ajax's performance during the 1970-1971 season, focusing on their playing style, results, and their ultimate league triumph. This season set the stage for their remarkable achievements in the following year, showcasing their growing confidence and the effectiveness of Total Football.

3. Total Football Unleashed: Ajax's Brilliance on Display

The 1971-1972 Eredivisie season witnessed Ajax's Total Football philosophy in full flow. We analyze their dominant performances, highlighting their attacking prowess, positional interchangeability, and collective brilliance. From the scintillating goals to the seamless transitions between defense and attack, Ajax's football was a spectacle to behold. We also explore the impact of key players such as Johan Cruyff, Johan Neeskens, and Arie Haan, who personified the spirit of Total Football on the domestic stage.

4. Rivalries and Challenges: Battling the Best

Ajax's dominance in the Eredivisie did not go unchallenged. We examine the rivalries and competitive battles they faced from other top Dutch clubs during the 1971-1972 season. Feyenoord, PSV Eindhoven, and other formidable opponents pushed Ajax to their limits, providing thrilling encounters and testing the mettle of Michels' men. We delve into the defining matches, the tactical battles, and the intense competition that shaped Ajax's journey to the Eredivisie title.

5. Setting Records and Breaking Barriers

Ajax's domination of the Eredivisie during the treble-winning season resulted in several records and milestones. We highlight the records set by Ajax, including their unbeaten run, the highest-scoring matches, and the individual achievements of their players. Moreover, we examine the impact of their success on the Dutch football landscape, the enthusiasm it generated among fans, and the inspiration it provided for future generations.

Conclusion

Ajax Amsterdam's dominance of the Eredivisie during the 1971-1972 treble-winning season was a testament to their footballing excellence and the success of Total Football. Their performances captivated fans, shattered records, and left an indelible mark on Dutch football. The Eredivisie triumph served as a springboard for their European conquest and solidified their place among the footballing giants. Ajax's dominance in the domestic league showcased the culmination of their hard work, talent, and tactical brilliance, etching their name in the annals of Dutch football history.

The journey through the KNVB Cup

In the treble-winning season of 1971-1972, Ajax Amsterdam's quest for glory extended beyond the Eredivisie and the UEFA Champions League. This chapter explores Ajax's memorable journey through the KNVB Cup, the premier domestic cup competition in the Netherlands. We delve into the challenges they faced, the exhilarating matches, and the defining moments that led them to triumph in this prestigious tournament.

1. The Significance of the KNVB Cup

To understand Ajax's journey through the KNVB Cup, we must first grasp the significance of this esteemed competition in Dutch football. We explore the history and tradition of the KNVB Cup, its role in shaping the national football landscape, and its standing within Ajax's quest for domestic dominance. This sets the stage for the club's pursuit of cup glory during the treble-winning season.

2. The Early Rounds: Navigating the Path

Ajax's journey through the KNVB Cup began with the early rounds, where they faced lower division teams and local rivals. We delve into the challenges posed by these matchups, analyzing Ajax's approach and the standout performances that propelled them to the later stages. Despite being favorites, Ajax encountered spirited opposition and had to demonstrate their superiority to advance.

3. Memorable Encounters: Tests of Resilience

As Ajax progressed through the rounds of the KNVB Cup, they encountered formidable opponents who pushed them to their limits. We highlight the memorable encounters and the tests of resilience Ajax faced during the knockout stages. From fiercely contested matches against fellow top-flight teams to dramatic encounters with underdogs, we unravel the thrilling narratives and pivotal moments that defined Ajax's cup run.

4. Semifinals and Final: Climaxing in Glory

The semifinals and final of the KNVB Cup provided the ultimate stage for Ajax to showcase their mettle and secure the domestic silverware. We analyze the semifinal matchups, dissecting the tactical battles and key performances that saw Ajax overcome their opponents. Then, we delve into the highly anticipated final, exploring the build-up, the atmosphere, and the high-stakes encounter that culminated in Ajax's quest for cup glory.

5. Total Football's Influence in the KNVB Cup

Throughout Ajax's journey in the KNVB Cup, the influence of Total Football was palpable. We examine how the club's revolutionary playing style, characterized by fluidity, tactical flexibility, and attacking brilliance, influenced their approach to cup matches. We explore the role of positional interchangeability, pressing, and collective responsibility in Ajax's success, highlighting the seamless integration of Total Football principles in their cup performances.

6. The Impact and Legacy of Ajax's KNVB Cup Triumph

Ajax's victory in the KNVB Cup during the treble-winning season left an indelible impact on the club's legacy and the wider footballing community. We explore the significance of this triumph, its celebration by the fans, and the enduring legacy it created within Dutch football. Additionally, we discuss the influence of Ajax's cup success on their subsequent campaigns and the inspiration it provided for future generations of players and teams.

Conclusion

Ajax Amsterdam's journey through the KNVB Cup during the 1971-1972 treble-winning season was filled with drama, excitement, and triumph. Their ability to navigate the early rounds, overcome challenging opponents, and ultimately secure the cup was a testament to their footballing prowess and the influence of Total Football. The KNVB Cup triumph added another chapter to Ajax's historic campaign and solidified their place among the footballing elite.

The captivating run in the UEFA Champions League

In the treble-winning season of 1971-1972, Ajax Amsterdam's quest for greatness extended beyond domestic competitions. This chapter delves into Ajax's captivating run in the UEFA Champions League, where they showcased their skill, tactical brilliance, and the revolutionary Total Football philosophy. We explore the challenges they faced, the iconic matches, and the unforgettable moments that defined their journey to European glory.

1. The UEFA Champions League: A Quest for European Supremacy

To understand the magnitude of Ajax's run in the UEFA Champions League, we must first explore the history and significance of the tournament. We examine the evolution of the European Cup into the Champions League, its allure for top clubs, and Ajax's aspirations to conquer the continent. This provides the backdrop for their compelling campaign in the 1971-1972 season.

2. The Group Stage: Overcoming Initial Hurdles

Ajax's journey in the Champions League began in the group stage, where they faced other elite European clubs. We analyze the challenges they encountered, the tactical battles, and the standout performances that propelled them to the knockout rounds. Despite being tested by formidable opponents, Ajax displayed their dominance and hinted at the brilliance that awaited in the later stages.

3. Quarterfinals and Semifinals: Defining Moments

The knockout rounds of the Champions League provided the stage for Ajax's defining moments. We delve into the quarterfinals and semifinals, exploring the matchups, tactical intricacies, and remarkable performances that saw Ajax overcome their opponents. From thrilling comebacks to emphatic victories, we unravel the narratives that propelled Ajax closer to their ultimate goal.

4. The Final: Triumph in Rotterdam

The UEFA Champions League final was the pinnacle of Ajax's campaign, where they aimed to be crowned champions of Europe. We delve into the build-up, the atmosphere, and the historic encounter that unfolded in Rotterdam. From the tactical battles to the individual brilliance, we dissect the final, highlighting the key moments that secured Ajax's triumph and cemented their place in footballing history.

5. Total Football's Influence on the European Stage

Ajax's captivating run in the Champions League showcased the influence of Total Football on the European stage. We examine how their revolutionary playing style, characterized by fluidity, positional interchangeability, and attacking prowess, confounded their opponents and captivated football fans. We analyze the impact of Total Football principles on Ajax's performances, highlighting the collective brilliance and individual brilliance of players such as Johan Cruyff and Johan Neeskens.

6. Legacy and Impact: The Aftermath of European Glory

Ajax's triumph in the UEFA Champions League during the treble-winning season left an enduring impact on the club, its fans, and the wider footballing world. We explore the significance of this historic achievement, the celebration by Ajax's loyal supporters, and the lasting legacy it created within Dutch and European football. Additionally, we discuss the influence of Ajax's success on subsequent Champions League campaigns and the inspiration it provided for future generations of players and clubs.

Conclusion

Ajax Amsterdam's captivating run in the UEFA Champions League during the 1971-1972 treble-winning season was a testament to their footballing excellence and the power of Total Football. Their journey to European glory showcased their skill, tactical brilliance, and unwavering determination. The triumph in the Champions League solidified Ajax's place among the footballing giants and left an indelible mark on the European football landscape.

The final triumph and memorable performances

The treble-winning season of 1971-1972 reached its zenith for Ajax Amsterdam with their crowning moment of glory in the final of the UEFA Champions League. This chapter delves into the final triumph and the unforgettable performances that defined Ajax's journey to European supremacy. We explore the build-up to the final, the iconic match itself, and the key individuals who shone brightest on the grandest stage.

1. The Road to the Final: Overcoming European Giants

Before delving into the final itself, we recap Ajax's path through the knockout stages of the UEFA Champions League. We examine the opponents they faced, the challenges encountered, and the defining moments that propelled them to the pinnacle of European football. From memorable victories over European giants to stunning displays of skill and tactical mastery, Ajax's journey to the final was marked by their unwavering commitment to Total Football.

2. The Final Venue: Feyenoord Stadion and the Stage Is Set

The choice of Feyenoord Stadion in Rotterdam as the venue for the final added a layer of intrigue and intensity to the showdown. We explore the significance of playing in their domestic rivals' stadium, the atmosphere generated by both sets of supporters, and the emotions running high on the day of the final. The stage was set for an enthralling encounter that would etch itself into footballing lore.

3. The Tactical Battle: Rinus Michels vs. Jupp Heynckes

The final pitted Ajax against Bayern Munich, and beyond the clash of two formidable teams, it also brought together two visionary coaches: Rinus Michels and Jupp Heynckes. We delve into the tactical battle between these masterminds, examining their approaches, strategic adjustments, and the cat-and-mouse game that unfolded on the field. The clash of philosophies added an extra dimension to the final spectacle.

4. Memorable Performances: Icons Shine Bright

The final witnessed memorable performances from individuals who stepped up when it mattered most. We analyze the standout displays of key players on both sides, delving into their impact on the match and their contributions to Ajax's triumph. From Johan Cruyff's mesmerizing skills and leadership to Arie Haan's crucial goals and the defensive brilliance of Ruud Krol and Barry

Hulshoff, we celebrate the heroes who paved the way to victory.

5. The Decisive Moments: Goals, Drama, and Glory

The final was replete with decisive moments that swung the balance in Ajax's favor. We unravel the drama, reliving the goals, near misses, and game-changing incidents that unfolded throughout the match. From stunning strikes to tactical switches and pivotal saves, each moment contributed to the narrative of Ajax's triumph and etched itself into the memories of players and fans alike.

6. The Aftermath: Celebrating European Supremacy

The final whistle marked the culmination of Ajax's treble-winning season and ignited scenes of jubilation and celebration. We delve into the aftermath of their European triumph, exploring the reactions of the players, the outpouring of joy from the fans, and the recognition of Ajax's historic achievement within the footballing community. We also discuss the lasting impact of their European success and its significance in the club's storied history.

Conclusion

Ajax Amsterdam's final triumph in the UEFA Champions League during the treble-winning season of 1971-1972 was a crowning achievement that sealed their place among the footballing immortals. Their unforgettable performances, individual brilliance, and tactical mastery culminated in a victory that echoed through the ages. The final showcased the essence of Ajax's Total Football philosophy and solidified their status as European champions, leaving an indelible mark on the club's history and inspiring future generations of players and teams.

Chapter 2: FC Barcelona - Season: 2008-2009
The era of Pep Guardiola and the transformation of Barcelona

The 2008-2009 season marked a turning point in the history of FC Barcelona, as the club experienced a remarkable transformation under the guidance of manager Pep Guardiola. This chapter explores the era of Guardiola and the profound impact he had on Barcelona's playing style, success, and identity. We delve into the tactical revolution, the team's philosophy, and the key elements that defined Guardiola's reign.

1. Pep Guardiola: A Managerial Visionary

To understand the era of Guardiola, we delve into the background and coaching philosophy of the man himself. We explore Guardiola's upbringing, his playing career at Barcelona, and his subsequent development as a coach. We analyze the key influences on his managerial style and his deep understanding of Barcelona's footballing DNA, which laid the foundation for the transformational era to come.

2. Total Football Reinvented: The Tactical Revolution

Guardiola's arrival heralded a tactical revolution at Barcelona, as he redefined the concept of Total Football for the modern era. We examine the key principles of Guardiola's playing style, including positional play, pressing, and fluidity. Through meticulous analysis, we unravel the tactical nuances that enabled Barcelona to dominate matches, control possession, and unleash devastating attacking prowess.

3. Building the Dream Team: The Evolution of Barcelona's Squad

Guardiola's vision required a squad that could execute his tactical blueprint. We trace the evolution of Barcelona's team during this era, highlighting key signings, departures, and the emergence of homegrown talents. From the backbone of the team featuring the likes of Carles Puyol and Xavi Hernández to the iconic trio of Lionel Messi, Andrés Iniesta, and Xavi, we examine how Guardiola shaped a squad that perfectly embodied his philosophy.

4. La Liga Supremacy: A Season of Dominance

The 2008-2009 season saw Barcelona assert their dominance in La Liga under Guardiola's guidance. We analyze their relentless pursuit of domestic success, the tactical strategies employed, and the memorable performances that showcased the team's evolution. From breathtaking attacking displays to solid defensive organization, we dissect the key matches and moments that propelled Barcelona to the summit of Spanish football.

5. Conquering the Copa del Rey: The Pursuit of Domestic Glory

In addition to their league triumph, Barcelona's hunger for success extended to the Copa del Rey. We delve into their campaign in the domestic cup competition, analyzing the challenges faced, standout performances, and the path to lifting the trophy. The pursuit of domestic glory further solidified Barcelona's status as the team to beat, setting the stage for their European quest.

6. The UEFA Champions League: Triumph in Rome

The ultimate test of Barcelona's transformation came in the UEFA Champions League. We relive their captivating run in the tournament, from the group stages to the historic final in Rome. We dissect the tactical battles, the mesmerizing displays of individual brilliance, and the defining moments that culminated in a memorable victory over Manchester United. Guardiola's Barcelona showcased their footballing philosophy on the grandest stage, leaving an indelible mark on the competition's history.

7. The Guardiola Effect: Legacy and Impact

Guardiola's era at Barcelona left a lasting impact on the club, its players, and the footballing world at large. We examine the legacy of his reign, discussing how Barcelona's style of play influenced the game and inspired other teams.

We also explore the personal growth of individual players under Guardiola's guidance and the long-lasting effects of his managerial approach on their careers.

Conclusion

The era of Pep Guardiola at FC Barcelona during the 2008-2009 season marked a period of unprecedented success and transformation. Through his tactical revolution and unwavering commitment to a distinct playing style, Guardiola molded Barcelona into an unstoppable force. The team's dominance in La Liga, triumph in the Copa del Rey, and victory in the UEFA Champions League symbolized the zenith of their transformation. Guardiola's legacy at Barcelona remains etched in the annals of footballing history, inspiring future generations and forever associating the club with a brand of football that captured the imagination of fans worldwide.

The battle for La Liga supremacy

In the 2008-2009 season, FC Barcelona embarked on a captivating journey to reclaim their status as the dominant force in Spanish football. This chapter focuses on the intense battle for La Liga supremacy, as Barcelona, under the guidance of Pep Guardiola, aimed to overthrow their rivals and reestablish their domestic dominance. We delve into the key matches, tactical strategies, and defining moments that shaped their successful campaign.

1. The Preseason Reinforcements: Building a Championship Squad

Before the battle for La Liga commenced, Barcelona made strategic reinforcements during the preseason to strengthen their squad. We explore the key signings, including Dani Alves and Gerard Piqué, and their impact on the team's defensive stability and attacking prowess. These additions, along with the existing core of players, set the stage for Barcelona's assault on the league title.

2. Guardiola's Tactical Revolution: Total Football Reborn

Guardiola implemented a tactical revolution at Barcelona, redefining the concept of Total Football for the modern era. We analyze the key principles of Guardiola's playing style, including positional play, pressing, and fluidity, and examine how these tactics were executed in the battle for La Liga. Barcelona's ability to control possession, suffocate opponents, and unleash devastating attacking moves became the hallmark of their quest for supremacy.

3. A Strong Start: Setting the Pace

Barcelona made an emphatic statement in the early stages of the season, setting the pace and sending a message to their rivals. We recount the crucial matches and standout performances that established Barcelona as the team to beat. From comprehensive victories to mesmerizing displays of skill, their dominance in the opening fixtures laid the foundation for their title challenge.

4. Rivalry Renewed: Clashes with Real Madrid

The battle for La Liga supremacy reached its peak in the encounters between Barcelona and their arch-rivals, Real Madrid. We analyze the highly anticipated clashes, dissecting the tactical strategies employed by both teams and the pivotal moments that decided the outcomes. These intense matches, featuring the likes of Lionel Messi, Cristiano Ronaldo, and Xavi Hernández, showcased the sheer intensity and quality of the rivalry.

5. Overcoming Challenges: A Test of Character

As the season progressed, Barcelona faced several challenges that tested their character and resolve. We delve into the matches against resolute opponents, where Barcelona had to dig deep to secure vital points. Whether it was battling against stubborn defenses, overcoming injuries, or responding to setbacks, these moments highlighted the mental strength and resilience of Guardiola's team.

6. Unleashing Messi: The Maestro's Magnificent Season

No discussion of Barcelona's battle for La Liga supremacy would be complete without highlighting the extraordinary performances of Lionel Messi. We analyze Messi's magnificent season, exploring his evolution as a player under Guardiola's guidance and his pivotal contributions in crucial matches. From breathtaking goals to sublime individual displays, Messi's brilliance became a driving force behind Barcelona's pursuit of the title.

7. The Decisive Stretch: Navigating the Crucial Phase

As the season neared its climax, Barcelona faced a defining stretch of matches that would determine their fate in the battle for La Liga. We examine the key fixtures during this period, discussing the tactical adjustments, the pressure-cooker atmosphere, and the unforgettable moments that propelled Barcelona closer to the championship. The ability to perform under immense pressure and deliver when it mattered most showcased the championship DNA of Guardiola's team.

8. Sealing the Title: Moments of Triumph

The battle for La Liga supremacy reached its culmination as Barcelona sealed the title. We relive the climactic moments, discussing the matches that ultimately secured their triumph. From iconic goals to collective displays of brilliance, these were the moments when Barcelona's dominance was cemented, and their reign as champions was assured.

Conclusion

The battle for La Liga supremacy during the 2008-2009 season epitomized Barcelona's transformation under Pep Guardiola. Through tactical innovation, mental fortitude, and the individual brilliance of players like Lionel Messi, Barcelona emerged victorious in their quest for domestic dominance. Their triumph in La Liga set the stage for further success and marked the beginning of a historic era for the club.

The pursuit of the Copa del Rey

In addition to their battle for La Liga supremacy, FC Barcelona's 2008-2009 season under the guidance of Pep Guardiola included a relentless pursuit of success in the Copa del Rey. This chapter delves into the team's campaign in the domestic cup competition, highlighting the challenges they faced, standout performances, and the path they took to lift the coveted trophy. We explore the significance of the Copa del Rey to Barcelona's season and the tactical strategies employed to secure victory.

1. The Importance of the Copa del Rey: A Shot at Domestic Glory

The Copa del Rey holds a special place in Spanish football, representing an opportunity for teams to secure domestic silverware and assert their dominance. We discuss the historical significance of the competition and its place within Barcelona's season. The pursuit of the Copa del Rey not only added to the club's trophy haul but also provided an avenue to showcase their depth of talent and hunger for success.

2. Squad Rotation and Depth: Managing the Demands

Competing on multiple fronts necessitated squad rotation and effective management of player fitness. We delve into Guardiola's approach to squad rotation during the

Copa del Rey campaign, examining the utilization of fringe players and the seamless integration of youth prospects. Barcelona's ability to maintain high standards despite rotating the squad reflected their depth of talent and the trust placed in every player.

3. Negotiating the Early Rounds: Overcoming Stubborn Opposition

The early rounds of the Copa del Rey often present unique challenges, with lower division teams proving to be resolute opponents. We analyze Barcelona's encounters with such opposition, highlighting the tactical approaches used to break down stubborn defenses and secure favorable results. These matches tested the team's creativity, adaptability, and mental resilience as they navigated their way through the early stages of the competition.

4. Clashes with Rivals: Intensity Amplified

The Copa del Rey frequently provides opportunities for heated encounters between rival clubs. We focus on Barcelona's matches against their traditional rivals, such as Real Madrid and Espanyol, where the stakes were raised and emotions ran high. These clashes showcased the intense nature of Spanish football rivalries and further fueled Barcelona's desire to claim the Copa del Rey as a statement of their superiority.

5. Semifinal Drama: A Battle to Reach the Final

The semifinal stage of the Copa del Rey often produces high-stakes, tightly contested matches. We recount Barcelona's semifinal battles, analyzing the key moments, tactical adjustments, and standout performances that propelled them closer to the final. Whether it was overcoming deficits, executing decisive strategies, or showcasing individual brilliance, these matches epitomized the drama and excitement associated with knockout football.

6. The Final Showdown: Sealing the Trophy

The journey in the Copa del Rey culminated in a climactic final, where Barcelona aimed to secure the trophy and add another chapter to their storied history. We relive the atmosphere, tension, and drama of the final match, analyzing the tactical battles, key incidents, and moments of individual brilliance that ultimately led to Barcelona's triumph. The final served as a fitting showcase of the team's progress under Guardiola and their unwavering pursuit of excellence.

7. The Significance of Copa del Rey Success: Adding to the Legacy

The Copa del Rey triumph held significance beyond the trophy itself. We discuss the importance of winning the competition in terms of Barcelona's season, the club's historical legacy, and the impact on the players' confidence and hunger for further success. The Copa del Rey victory served as a testament to Barcelona's depth, resilience, and ability to perform under pressure.

Conclusion

The pursuit of the Copa del Rey during the 2008-2009 season showcased Barcelona's relentless drive for domestic glory. Through squad rotation, tactical prowess, and standout performances, they overcame challenges and secured the coveted trophy. The Copa del Rey success not only added to Barcelona's trophy cabinet but also reinforced their status as a force to be reckoned with in Spanish football.

The mesmerizing UEFA Champions League campaign

FC Barcelona's 2008-2009 season under the guidance of Pep Guardiola was not only marked by their domestic dominance but also by their mesmerizing campaign in the UEFA Champions League. This chapter explores Barcelona's journey in Europe's premier club competition, highlighting their tactical brilliance, memorable performances, and the path they took to lift the coveted trophy. We delve into the significance of the Champions League to Barcelona's season and the impact of their style of play on the global stage.

1. The Quest for European Glory: Champions League as the Ultimate Prize

The UEFA Champions League stands as the pinnacle of club football, and Barcelona entered the tournament with ambitions of claiming European glory. We discuss the historical significance of the competition, the club's previous successes, and the importance of the Champions League to Barcelona's season. The quest for European supremacy provided the stage for Barcelona to showcase their unique brand of football to the world.

2. Group Stage Domination: Setting the Tone

Barcelona's Champions League campaign began in the group stage, where they aimed to establish their dominance early on. We analyze their performances in the group stage matches, highlighting their exceptional ball control, fluid passing, and attacking prowess. From resounding victories to memorable comebacks, Barcelona's performances set the tone for their mesmerizing run in the tournament.

3. Tactical Brilliance: Guardiola's Masterstrokes

Pep Guardiola's tactical brilliance came to the fore during Barcelona's Champions League campaign. We examine the strategic adjustments and innovative approaches employed by Guardiola, including the utilization of false nines, positional play, and high-intensity pressing. Barcelona's ability to control games, suffocate opponents, and unleash devastating attacking moves showcased the sheer brilliance of Guardiola's tactical masterstrokes.

4. Memorable Knockout Ties: Navigating the Challenges

The knockout stages of the Champions League present the most daunting challenges, as the continent's best teams vie for a place in the final. We recount Barcelona's memorable encounters in the knockout rounds, discussing the tactical battles, key moments, and standout performances that propelled them towards the trophy. From overcoming formidable opponents to displaying mental resilience, these ties demonstrated Barcelona's ability to rise to the occasion when it mattered most.

5. The Iconic Semi-Final: The Battle of the Titans

The Champions League semi-final witnessed a clash of titans as Barcelona faced off against a formidable opponent. We delve into the iconic semi-final match, analyzing the tactical strategies, individual brilliance, and decisive moments that unfolded. The atmosphere, intensity, and sheer quality of football on display in this match encapsulated the essence of the Champions League and showcased Barcelona's ability to perform at the highest level.

6. The Road to the Final: Moments of Brilliance

As Barcelona progressed through the knockout stages, they produced moments of brilliance that captivated football fans worldwide. We highlight these moments, whether it was a sublime individual goal, a breathtaking team move, or a game-changing intervention by a key player. These instances of brilliance not only propelled Barcelona towards the final but also added to the narrative of their mesmerizing Champions League campaign.

7. The Final Triumph: Cementing Greatness

The Champions League final represented the culmination of Barcelona's mesmerizing campaign. We relive the atmosphere, tension, and drama of the final match, discussing the tactical battles, key incidents, and moments of individual brilliance that led to Barcelona's triumph. The final served as a fitting showcase of Barcelona's quality, their unique style of play, and their ability to conquer Europe's finest clubs.

8. Impact and Legacy: Redefining Footballing Excellence

Barcelona's mesmerizing Champions League campaign had a lasting impact on the footballing landscape. We examine the influence of their playing style, tactical innovations, and collective brilliance on the evolution of the sport. Barcelona's success not only redefined the concept of footballing excellence but also left an indelible mark on subsequent generations of players, coaches, and clubs.

Conclusion

Barcelona's mesmerizing UEFA Champions League campaign during the 2008-2009 season showcased their tactical brilliance, individual talent, and unwavering commitment to their unique style of play. The journey towards European glory captured the hearts and minds of football fans worldwide and solidified Barcelona's place among the all-time great teams in the history of the Champions League.

The iconic final and the triumph of style

The pinnacle of FC Barcelona's remarkable 2008-2009 season was reached in the UEFA Champions League final, where they faced off against a formidable opponent. This chapter delves into the iconic final and the triumphant display of Barcelona's distinct style of play. We explore the tactical battles, individual brilliance, and memorable moments that defined the match and solidified Barcelona's place in footballing history. The final represented the culmination of their season-long efforts and served as a testament to their unwavering commitment to a unique brand of football.

1. Setting the Stage: The Road to the Final

Before delving into the final itself, we provide an overview of Barcelona's journey to reach the Champions League final. We recount the memorable matches, standout performances, and key moments that propelled them through the knockout stages. From group stage dominance to dramatic victories in the quarter-finals and semi-finals, Barcelona's path to the final demonstrated their prowess and set the stage for a thrilling showdown.

2. Tactical Showdown: Clash of Styles

The final pitted Barcelona against a formidable opponent with a contrasting style of play. We examine the tactical approaches of both teams, analyzing the strategies employed, positional battles, and the adjustments made throughout the match. The clash of styles heightened the intrigue and showcased the contrasting philosophies of the two clubs, setting the stage for a captivating encounter.

3. The Barcelona Style: Fluidity, Possession, and Creativity

At the heart of Barcelona's triumph in the final was their distinct style of play. We delve into the principles that defined Barcelona's style, including fluid positional play, relentless pressing, and intricate passing patterns. We explore the role of key players in executing this style, such as Xavi Hernández, Andrés Iniesta, and Lionel Messi, highlighting their contributions and the seamless coordination within the team.

4. Moments of Brilliance: Individual Heroics

While Barcelona's style of play was a collective effort, individual moments of brilliance played a crucial role in shaping the outcome of the final. We highlight the standout performances and memorable individual contributions that turned the tide in Barcelona's favor. From breathtaking goals to exquisite dribbles and game-changing interventions, these moments exemplified the exceptional skill and talent within the Barcelona ranks.

5. Tactical Adjustments: Outsmarting the Opposition

The final also witnessed tactical adjustments and strategic decisions that proved decisive in Barcelona's triumph. We analyze the key decisions made by Pep Guardiola and the coaching staff, such as substitutions, formation tweaks, and instructions to the players. These adjustments showcased Guardiola's tactical acumen and his ability to outmaneuver the opposition, ultimately leading to Barcelona's success on the grandest stage.

6. Decisive Moments: Shaping the Outcome

In any final, certain moments define the outcome of the match. We delve into the crucial incidents and decisive moments that shaped the final. Whether it was a game-changing goal, a crucial save, or a pivotal defensive intervention, these moments shifted the momentum in Barcelona's favor and added to the drama and intensity of the match.

7. The Triumph of Style: A Statement of Footballing Excellence

Barcelona's victory in the final was not just about lifting the trophy—it was a statement of footballing excellence. We discuss how their style of play, characterized by fluidity, possession, and creativity, came to fruition in the final. The triumph of style represented a vindication of

Barcelona's approach to the game and solidified their status as one of the greatest teams of their generation.

8. The Aftermath: Legacy and Inspiration

The iconic final and Barcelona's triumph of style left a lasting legacy in the footballing world. We explore the impact of their victory on subsequent generations of players, coaches, and clubs. From tactical imitations to a renewed focus on possession-oriented football, Barcelona's success inspired a new wave of footballing philosophy and left an indelible mark on the sport.

Conclusion

The iconic final of the 2008-2009 UEFA Champions League showcased Barcelona's triumph of style, where their distinct brand of football conquered the opposition and etched their name in footballing history. The tactical battles, individual brilliance, and decisive moments on that unforgettable night encapsulated the essence of Barcelona's season and served as a testament to their unwavering commitment to a unique style of play. The final represented the culmination of their journey and solidified their place among the pantheon of footballing greats.

Chapter 3: Bayern Munich - Season: 2019-2020
Bayern Munich's dominance in German football

Chapter 3 delves into Bayern Munich's remarkable season in 2019-2020, focusing on their dominance in German football. We explore the factors that contributed to their unparalleled success, including their squad strength, managerial excellence, and their ability to consistently outperform their rivals. This chapter highlights Bayern Munich's sheer dominance in the Bundesliga, their relentless pursuit of excellence, and their impact on German football as a whole.

1. The Bundesliga: Germany's Premier Football League

To understand Bayern Munich's dominance, it is crucial to provide an overview of the Bundesliga as Germany's premier football league. We discuss its history, structure, and the competitive landscape, highlighting the significance of winning the Bundesliga title. The league's rich history and passionate fan base set the stage for Bayern Munich's quest for supremacy.

2. The Rise of Bayern Munich: From Regional Powerhouse to National Dominance

We trace the evolution of Bayern Munich from a regional powerhouse to a dominant force in German football.

The club's early successes, strategic investments, and visionary leadership laid the foundation for their subsequent rise to dominance. We explore how Bayern Munich established themselves as a force to be reckoned with, both domestically and internationally.

3. The Appointment of Hansi Flick: Catalyst for Success

The appointment of Hansi Flick as head coach proved to be a turning point for Bayern Munich. We examine Flick's managerial credentials, his tactical approach, and his ability to inspire the players. Under Flick's guidance, Bayern Munich experienced a resurgence and reached new heights of performance and success.

4. Squad Depth and Strength: The Bavarian Powerhouse

One key aspect of Bayern Munich's dominance is their exceptional squad depth and strength. We analyze the club's transfer strategy, player recruitment, and the development of their youth academy. From established stars to emerging talents, Bayern Munich's squad boasted a remarkable blend of experience and potential, enabling them to maintain their high standards throughout the season.

5. Relentless Pursuit of Excellence: Consistency and Winning Mentality

Bayern Munich's dominance in German football can be attributed to their relentless pursuit of excellence. We discuss their winning mentality, their hunger for success, and their ability to consistently perform at a high level. The club's focus on continuous improvement, strong team dynamics, and a winning culture played a crucial role in their sustained dominance.

6. Record-Breaking Bundesliga Season: Setting New Standards

The 2019-2020 Bundesliga season witnessed Bayern Munich's record-breaking campaign. We delve into their exceptional performances, goal-scoring prowess, and defensive solidity. From their impressive winning streaks to their commanding goal differences, Bayern Munich set new standards in German football, rewriting the record books along the way.

7. Overcoming Challenges: Resilience in the Face of Adversity

Despite their dominance, Bayern Munich faced challenges and setbacks during the season. We explore how they navigated injuries, fixture congestion, and strong competition to maintain their grip on the Bundesliga title. Their ability to overcome adversity showcased their resilience and mental strength, further cementing their status as the dominant force in German football.

8. Impact on German Football: Raising the Bar

Bayern Munich's dominance in the Bundesliga had a profound impact on German football as a whole. We examine how their success raised the bar for other clubs, forcing them to improve and adapt. We also discuss the influence of Bayern Munich's dominance on the national team, youth development, and the overall reputation of German football on the international stage.

Conclusion

Bayern Munich's dominance in German football during the 2019-2020 season was a testament to their exceptional squad, managerial excellence, and relentless pursuit of excellence. Their record-breaking Bundesliga campaign not only solidified their status as the preeminent force in German football but also raised the bar for other clubs. Bayern Munich's impact on German football extends beyond their domestic success, inspiring a new era of competitiveness and driving the nation's footballing standards to new heights.

The Bundesliga triumph

Chapter 3 focuses on Bayern Munich's remarkable triumph in the Bundesliga during the 2019-2020 season. This section explores their dominance in the German top-flight, highlighting their exceptional performances, relentless pursuit of victory, and the key factors that contributed to their success. We delve into their record-breaking season, memorable matches, and the impact of their Bundesliga triumph on German football.

1. The Bundesliga Landscape: A Highly Competitive League

To understand the significance of Bayern Munich's triumph, we provide an overview of the Bundesliga landscape during the 2019-2020 season. We examine the competitive nature of the league, the challengers vying for the title, and the historical context of Bayern Munich's dominance. This sets the stage for understanding the magnitude of their achievement.

2. Building the Foundation: Preseason Preparation and Squad Evolution

We delve into Bayern Munich's preseason preparation and the strategic decisions that laid the foundation for their Bundesliga triumph. We discuss the club's transfer activities, squad evolution, and the integration of new signings. The meticulous planning and squad management played a crucial role in shaping Bayern Munich's title-winning campaign.

3. Dominating the League: Unparalleled Consistency

Bayern Munich's dominance in the Bundesliga was characterized by their unparalleled consistency. We analyze their impressive winning streaks, points tally, and goal-scoring prowess throughout the season. From their offensive firepower to defensive resilience, Bayern Munich's ability to maintain their high standards week in and week out set them apart from their rivals.

4. Tactical Brilliance: Flick's Impact and Tactical Adjustments

The appointment of Hansi Flick as head coach proved instrumental in Bayern Munich's Bundesliga triumph. We explore Flick's tactical approach, his ability to adapt to different opponents, and the strategic adjustments he made throughout the season. From high-pressing football to fluid positional play, Bayern Munich's tactical brilliance under Flick elevated their performances to new heights.

5. Memorable Matches: Key Moments in the Title Race

We highlight the memorable matches that shaped Bayern Munich's Bundesliga triumph. From crucial encounters against their closest rivals to dominant displays against challenging opponents, we examine the pivotal moments, standout performances, and game-changing goals that contributed to their success. These matches showcase Bayern Munich's ability to rise to the occasion and secure crucial victories when it mattered most.

6. Offensive Prowess: The Goalscoring Powerhouse

Bayern Munich's attacking prowess played a significant role in their Bundesliga triumph. We analyze their prolific goalscoring record, highlighting the contributions of key players such as Robert Lewandowski, Thomas Müller, and Serge Gnabry. From intricate build-up play to clinical finishing, Bayern Munich's offensive firepower overwhelmed their opponents and propelled them towards the title.

7. Defensive Solidity: The Backbone of Success

While Bayern Munich's attacking prowess often took the spotlight, their defensive solidity was equally crucial to their triumph. We examine the defensive organization, the contributions of individual defenders, and the leadership of Manuel Neuer in goal. Bayern Munich's ability to limit their opponents' scoring opportunities and maintain a disciplined defensive structure fortified their title-winning campaign.

8. Overcoming Challenges: Resilience and Mental Strength

Throughout the season, Bayern Munich faced various challenges and setbacks. We discuss how they overcame injuries, fixture congestion, and moments of adversity. The team's resilience, mental strength, and ability to bounce back from setbacks were essential factors in their ability to maintain their focus and emerge as Bundesliga champions.

9. Setting Records: Rewriting Bundesliga History

Bayern Munich's triumph in the 2019-2020 Bundesliga season was accompanied by a series of record-breaking achievements. We highlight the records they set, including the most goals scored in a single season, the largest goal difference, and the highest points tally. Bayern Munich's record-breaking campaign solidified their place in Bundesliga history and elevated their status as one of the greatest teams in German football.

Conclusion

Bayern Munich's Bundesliga triumph during the 2019-2020 season was a testament to their exceptional consistency, tactical brilliance, offensive prowess, and defensive solidity. Their ability to dominate the league, overcome challenges, and set new records showcased their superiority in German football. Bayern Munich's triumph not only secured them the Bundesliga title but also left an indelible mark on the league's history, establishing them as the standard-bearers of excellence in German football.

The DFB-Pokal journey

Chapter 3 explores Bayern Munich's journey in the DFB-Pokal during the 2019-2020 season. This section focuses on their pursuit of the prestigious domestic cup competition, highlighting the challenges they faced, memorable matches, and the ultimate triumph. We delve into Bayern Munich's relentless quest for silverware, their squad depth, tactical brilliance, and the impact of their DFB-Pokal success.

1. The Significance of the DFB-Pokal: Germany's Premier Domestic Cup

To understand the significance of Bayern Munich's journey, we provide an overview of the DFB-Pokal as Germany's premier domestic cup competition. We discuss its historical importance, the allure of the tournament, and the participation of clubs from various tiers of German football. The DFB-Pokal represents an opportunity for clubs to showcase their abilities and compete for silverware.

2. Building on Success: Bayern Munich's Cup Pedigree

We explore Bayern Munich's rich history in the DFB-Pokal and their pedigree in domestic cup competitions. We discuss their previous triumphs, memorable cup runs, and the club's tradition of success. Bayern Munich's experience and winning mentality laid the foundation for their pursuit of glory in the 2019-2020 season.

3. Squad Rotation and Depth: Navigating the Demands of Cup Competitions

Bayern Munich's success in the DFB-Pokal can be attributed to their squad rotation and depth. We analyze how the club managed their resources, providing opportunities to fringe players while maintaining a competitive edge. The depth of Bayern Munich's squad allowed them to navigate the demands of cup competitions without compromising their chances of success.

4. Early Rounds: Negotiating Lower-League Opponents

In the early rounds of the DFB-Pokal, Bayern Munich faced lower-league opponents. We delve into their matches against these teams, exploring the challenges they posed and Bayern Munich's ability to assert their dominance. Despite being heavy favorites, Bayern Munich had to navigate potential upsets and demonstrate their professionalism to progress in the tournament.

5. Fierce Battles: Overcoming Bundesliga Rivals

As the competition progressed, Bayern Munich faced fellow Bundesliga rivals in intense cup battles. We examine the matchups against strong opponents, analyzing the tactical duels, key moments, and standout performances. These matches tested Bayern Munich's mettle and showcased their ability to rise to the occasion against familiar adversaries.

6. Semifinals: Navigating High-Stakes Encounters

The semifinals of the DFB-Pokal represented a crucial stage in Bayern Munich's journey. We highlight the semifinal match, discussing the opposition, the significance of the encounter, and the tactical approach adopted by Bayern Munich. The high-stakes nature of these matches required Bayern Munich to showcase their mental strength and composure under pressure.

7. The Final Showdown: Pursuit of Cup Glory

The DFB-Pokal final was the culmination of Bayern Munich's journey. We provide a detailed account of the final match, analyzing the opposition, the tactical battle, and the memorable moments that unfolded. The final represented a chance for Bayern Munich to secure domestic cup glory and cement their status as the dominant force in German football.

8. The Sweet Taste of Victory: Celebrating the DFB-Pokal Triumph

We explore the aftermath of Bayern Munich's DFB-Pokal triumph, examining the celebrations, the significance of the trophy, and the impact on the club and its fans. The victory in the DFB-Pokal added another trophy to Bayern Munich's impressive haul and solidified their reputation as a serial winner in German football.

Conclusion

Bayern Munich's journey in the DFB-Pokal during the 2019-2020 season was a testament to their squad depth, tactical acumen, and ability to navigate the challenges of cup competitions. Their success in the tournament highlighted their dominance in German football and added to their legacy of triumphs. The DFB-Pokal journey exemplified Bayern Munich's hunger for silverware and their relentless pursuit of excellence in all competitions.

The UEFA Champions League run

Chapter 3 focuses on Bayern Munich's memorable UEFA Champions League run during the 2019-2020 season. This section delves into the challenges they faced, the iconic matches they played, and the ultimate triumph in Europe's most prestigious club competition. We explore the tactical brilliance, individual performances, and the indomitable spirit that propelled Bayern Munich to European glory.

1. The UEFA Champions League: The Holy Grail of European Club Football

To set the stage, we provide an overview of the UEFA Champions League and its significance in the world of football. We discuss the competition's history, its allure, and the prestige associated with lifting the coveted trophy. The UEFA Champions League represents the pinnacle of club football, and Bayern Munich's journey in the 2019-2020 season epitomized the pursuit of European glory.

2. Building on Past Success: Bayern Munich's European Pedigree

We delve into Bayern Munich's illustrious history in the UEFA Champions League, highlighting their previous triumphs and notable campaigns. We explore their stature as one of Europe's most successful clubs and discuss how their past successes laid the foundation for their aspirations in the 2019-2020 season.

3. Navigating the Group Stage: Early Hurdles and Dominance

Bayern Munich's UEFA Champions League run began in the group stage. We analyze their performances and results, discussing the challenges they faced and their dominance in the early matches. The group stage served as a platform for Bayern Munich to establish their credentials and build momentum for the knockout rounds.

4. Round of 16: Overcoming Adversity and Advancing

In the round of 16, Bayern Munich faced a formidable opponent. We delve into the matchup, analyzing the tactical battles, key moments, and the resilience displayed by Bayern Munich. Overcoming adversity and advancing to the quarterfinals showcased their mental fortitude and determination to go far in the competition.

5. Quarterfinals: Showdowns with European Giants

The quarterfinal stage pitted Bayern Munich against a fellow European powerhouse. We explore the tactical encounters, the drama, and the memorable performances that unfolded. These matches tested Bayern Munich's mettle and showcased their ability to rise to the occasion against top-tier opposition.

6. Semifinals: Battles for a Spot in the Final

The semifinals represented a crucial stage in Bayern Munich's UEFA Champions League journey. We highlight the matchups, analyzing the tactical duels, key moments, and standout performances. The intensity of the semifinals required Bayern Munich to display their best football and showcase their ability to perform under pressure.

7. The Final Showdown: European Glory Beckons

The UEFA Champions League final was the pinnacle of Bayern Munich's journey. We provide a detailed account of the final match, discussing the opposition, the tactical approach, and the iconic moments that unfolded. The final represented a chance for Bayern Munich to claim European glory and etch their names in the history books.

8. The Triumph and Its Significance: European Domination

We explore the aftermath of Bayern Munich's UEFA Champions League triumph, examining the celebrations, the impact on the club and its fans, and the significance of lifting the trophy. Bayern Munich's victory solidified their status as one of Europe's elite clubs and showcased their dominance on the continental stage.

Conclusion

Bayern Munich's UEFA Champions League run in the 2019-2020 season was a remarkable journey marked by exceptional performances, tactical brilliance, and unwavering determination. Their triumph in Europe's most prestigious club competition reaffirmed their status as a football powerhouse and added another chapter to their storied history. The UEFA Champions League run exemplified Bayern Munich's ability to rise to the occasion, overcome challenges, and achieve greatness on the continental stage.

The triumphant final and the treble glory

Chapter 3 explores the crowning moment of Bayern Munich's remarkable 2019-2020 season: the triumphant final of the UEFA Champions League and the club's attainment of the treble. We delve into the significance of the final match, the team's extraordinary performance, and the lasting impact of Bayern Munich's treble-winning campaign.

1. Setting the Stage: The Importance of the Final

To contextualize Bayern Munich's triumphant final, we highlight the significance of the match within the club's season and European football as a whole. We discuss the anticipation and excitement surrounding the final, the historical context of the club's previous achievements, and the weight of the treble at stake.

2. The Road to the Final: Reflecting on the Journey

We reflect on Bayern Munich's path to the final, recounting the memorable matches, defining moments, and standout performances that brought them to the brink of European glory. We examine the team's resilience, tactical prowess, and their ability to navigate the challenges posed by formidable opponents along the way.

3. The Opponent: A Worthy Challenge

We analyze the opponent Bayern Munich faced in the final, discussing their strengths, tactics, and previous performances in the competition. We highlight the significance of the matchup and the tactical considerations Bayern Munich had to address in order to secure victory.

4. Tactical Brilliance: Mastering the Final

We delve into the tactical aspects of the final, exploring Bayern Munich's approach, key strategic decisions, and the contributions of the players on the field. We analyze the team's formation, style of play, and how they effectively neutralized their opponent's threats while capitalizing on their own strengths.

5. Memorable Moments: Goals, Drama, and Highlights

We recount the memorable moments that unfolded during the final, including crucial goals, pivotal incidents, and instances of individual brilliance. We highlight the impact of standout performances by Bayern Munich players and the decisive moments that shaped the outcome of the match.

6. The Triumph of Style: A Showcase of Dominance

We discuss how Bayern Munich's victory in the final exemplified their style of play and their dominance throughout the season. We explore their attacking prowess, defensive solidity, and the collective effort that led to their success. We analyze the fluidity of their play, the precision of their passing, and the relentless pressure they applied on their opponent.

7. Celebrating the Treble: Impact and Legacy

We examine the significance of Bayern Munich's achievement of the treble, winning the Bundesliga, DFB-Pokal, and the UEFA Champions League in a single season. We discuss the impact of this historic feat on the club, the fans, and the wider footballing world. We also explore the legacy it has left behind and its lasting influence on subsequent generations.

Conclusion

The triumphant final and the treble glory of Bayern Munich in the 2019-2020 season encapsulated the club's exceptional performances, tactical brilliance, and unwavering determination. The final was a showcase of their dominance and a testament to their ability to rise to the occasion. Bayern Munich's treble-winning campaign will forever be remembered as a defining moment in the club's illustrious history, solidifying their status as one of Europe's greatest football teams.

Chapter 4: Legends and Key Figures
Exploring the legendary figures associated with each club

Chapter 5 delves into the iconic individuals who have left an indelible mark on the treble-winning seasons of Ajax Amsterdam, FC Barcelona, and Bayern Munich. This chapter explores the legendary figures associated with each club, highlighting their contributions, defining moments, and lasting legacies. From players to coaches, administrators to supporters, we celebrate the personalities who have shaped the history and success of these great European football clubs.

1. Ajax Amsterdam's Legends: Pioneers of Total Football

We begin by exploring the legendary figures associated with Ajax Amsterdam, the Dutch powerhouse that pioneered the concept of Total Football. We delve into the influence of players such as Johan Cruyff, the epitome of Total Football, and his impact on the club's playing style and success. We also highlight the contributions of other key figures, including Rinus Michels, the innovative coach, and club legends like Marco van Basten and Dennis Bergkamp.

2. FC Barcelona's Iconic Figures: The Architects of Tiki-Taka

Next, we turn our attention to FC Barcelona, a club known for its mesmerizing style of play, commonly referred to as Tiki-Taka. We explore the pivotal role of legendary players like Lionel Messi, who symbolizes the club's excellence and creative genius. We also discuss the influence of iconic coaches such as Pep Guardiola, who revolutionized the team's tactical approach. Additionally, we shine a light on other prominent figures, including Johan Cruyff, Xavi Hernandez, and Andres Iniesta, who have shaped the club's identity and success.

3. Bayern Munich's Heroes: The Bavarian Legends

In this section, we celebrate the legendary figures associated with Bayern Munich, the dominant force in German football. We examine the contributions of players like Franz Beckenbauer, who not only excelled on the field but also became influential figures off the pitch. We discuss the achievements of Gerd Muller, the prolific goalscorer, and the impact of coaches like Jupp Heynckes and Uli Hoeness. Additionally, we highlight the significance of key personalities in the club's administration and fan base.

4. Defining Moments and Memorable Contributions

In this section, we highlight the defining moments and memorable contributions of these legendary figures. We discuss their standout performances, historic goals, leadership qualities, and the impact they had on their respective clubs' treble-winning seasons. We analyze their influence on the team's playing style, tactics, and overall success, and how their achievements continue to resonate in the hearts of fans.

5. Legacy and Influence

We conclude the chapter by examining the lasting legacy and influence of these legendary figures. We explore how their contributions have shaped the clubs' histories and identities. We discuss their impact on subsequent generations of players, the inspiration they provided to aspiring footballers, and their influence on the development of the game itself. We also highlight the recognition and accolades they have received, solidifying their status as icons of European football.

Conclusion

The legendary figures associated with each club have played an instrumental role in the treble-winning seasons of Ajax Amsterdam, FC Barcelona, and Bayern Munich. This chapter has explored the iconic players, coaches, administrators, and supporters who have left an indelible mark on their respective clubs' histories. Their contributions, both on and off the field, have defined eras, shaped playing styles, and inspired generations of football enthusiasts. Their legacy continues to reverberate through the annals of European football, reminding us of the greatness that can be achieved by those who embody passion, skill, and determination.

The impact of iconic players, coaches, and key personnel

Chapter 5 explores the significant impact of iconic players, coaches, and key personnel associated with the treble-winning seasons of Ajax Amsterdam, FC Barcelona, and Bayern Munich. This section delves into the remarkable contributions and influence of these individuals, highlighting their role in shaping the success and legacy of their respective clubs. From inspirational leaders on the field to visionary tacticians on the sidelines, we examine how these figures propelled their teams to greatness and left an indelible mark on European football.

1. Iconic Players: Masters of their Craft

1.1 Ajax Amsterdam's Player Icons

We begin by exploring the impact of iconic players from Ajax Amsterdam. We delve into the legacy of Johan Cruyff, the embodiment of Total Football, and his revolutionary influence on the game. We also examine the contributions of players like Marco van Basten, Dennis Bergkamp, and Johan Neeskens, who played pivotal roles in Ajax's treble-winning season. Their exceptional skills, tactical understanding, and ability to deliver on the biggest stages made them true legends of the game.

1.2 FC Barcelona's Player Icons

Next, we turn our attention to FC Barcelona and the iconic players who have left an indelible mark on the club's treble-winning campaigns. Lionel Messi takes center stage as we explore his unmatched talent, incredible goal-scoring prowess, and transformative impact on the team. We also highlight the contributions of players like Xavi Hernandez, Andres Iniesta, and Ronaldinho, who were instrumental in Barcelona's success during these seasons. Their technical brilliance, vision, and ability to control the game elevated the club to new heights.

1.3 Bayern Munich's Player Icons

In this section, we examine the impact of iconic players at Bayern Munich. We delve into the legacy of players like Franz Beckenbauer, who epitomized elegance and leadership both on and off the field. Gerd Muller's lethal goal-scoring ability and his knack for finding the back of the net are also highlighted. We also discuss the contributions of other legendary players such as Oliver Kahn, Philipp Lahm, and Bastian Schweinsteiger, who played integral roles in Bayern's treble-winning season. Their skills, determination, and commitment to excellence set them apart as true icons of the game.

2. Visionary Coaches: Masterminds Behind Success

2.1 Ajax Amsterdam's Coaching Icons

We delve into the impact of visionary coaches associated with Ajax Amsterdam's treble-winning season. Rinus Michels, the architect of Total Football, is celebrated for his innovative tactics and ability to instill a cohesive playing style within the team. We also discuss the influence of other notable coaches, including Louis van Gaal and Johan Cruyff, who continued to build on the club's philosophy and achieve further success. Their strategic acumen, man-management skills, and commitment to developing young talents shaped Ajax's identity and propelled the team to greatness.

2.2 FC Barcelona's Coaching Icons

Next, we analyze the impact of visionary coaches at FC Barcelona. Pep Guardiola's tenure stands out as a transformative period in the club's history. We explore his tactical innovations, emphasis on possession-based football, and his ability to nurture young talents. We also discuss the contributions of other influential coaches such as Johan Cruyff, Frank Rijkaard, and Luis Enrique, who each played a significant role in shaping Barcelona's success during their respective treble-winning seasons. Their coaching philosophies, ability to inspire their players, and unwavering commitment to attacking football established Barcelona as a dominant force in European football.

2.3 Bayern Munich's Coaching Icons

In this section, we delve into the impact of visionary coaches at Bayern Munich. We highlight the influence of coaches like Jupp Heynckes, who guided the team to their treble-winning season. We analyze his tactical prowess, man-management skills, and ability to create a winning mentality within the squad. We also discuss the contributions of other notable coaches such as Ottmar Hitzfeld, Louis van Gaal, and Hansi Flick, who each left their mark on the club's history and contributed to their success. Their strategic brilliance, ability to motivate their players, and attention to detail ensured Bayern Munich's continued dominance in German football.

Conclusion

Chapter 5 has explored the impact of iconic players, coaches, and key personnel associated with the treble-winning seasons of Ajax Amsterdam, FC Barcelona, and Bayern Munich. From legendary players who mesmerized audiences with their skills to visionary coaches who revolutionized the game, these individuals have left an indelible mark on their clubs' histories and the wider football landscape. Their contributions have shaped the identity and success of their respective teams, inspiring future generations and ensuring their legacy lives on.

The memorable contributions and defining moments

Chapter 5 delves into the remarkable contributions and defining moments of the legends and key figures associated with the treble-winning seasons of Ajax Amsterdam, FC Barcelona, and Bayern Munich. This section explores the memorable performances, game-changing decisions, and iconic moments that shaped the success and legacy of these individuals. From crucial goals to tactical masterstrokes, we delve into the instances that solidified their status as legendary figures in European football.

1. Ajax Amsterdam: Memorable Contributions and Defining Moments

1.1 Johan Cruyff's Total Football Legacy

We begin with the legendary Johan Cruyff and his memorable contributions to Ajax Amsterdam's treble-winning season. We explore his pivotal role in popularizing the concept of Total Football, showcasing his exceptional skills, vision, and ability to dictate play. We delve into defining moments, such as his sublime performances in key matches and his influence on the team's playing style. From his iconic "Cruyff turn" to his leadership on and off the field, we celebrate the indelible mark Cruyff left on Ajax's success.

1.2 Marco van Basten's Goal-Scoring Brilliance

Next, we focus on the memorable contributions of Marco van Basten during Ajax's treble-winning campaign. We highlight his incredible goal-scoring prowess, analyzing his crucial goals in decisive matches and his ability to deliver under pressure. We also examine standout moments, such as his acrobatic volley in the UEFA European Championship final and his clinical finishing throughout the season. Van Basten's goal-scoring exploits and his ability to make a difference in crucial moments solidify his legendary status.

1.3 Dennis Bergkamp's Artistry and Technique

In this section, we explore Dennis Bergkamp's memorable contributions to Ajax Amsterdam's success. We delve into his exceptional technique, ball control, and creative playmaking abilities that made him a standout figure during the treble-winning season. We analyze his decisive goals, such as his memorable strike against Real Madrid in the UEFA Champions League, and his ability to create scoring opportunities for his teammates. Bergkamp's artistry and impact on the pitch cement his place among Ajax's legendary figures.

1.4 Johan Neeskens' Tenacity and Tactical Acumen

Lastly, we examine Johan Neeskens' memorable contributions to Ajax's triumph. We highlight his tenacity, versatility, and tactical understanding that made him an indispensable asset to the team. We explore his influential performances in midfield, his ability to control the game's tempo, and his crucial contributions in both defense and attack. Neeskens' combative spirit and tactical acumen played a pivotal role in Ajax's success, establishing him as a key figure in the treble-winning season.

2. FC Barcelona: Memorable Contributions and Defining Moments

2.1 Lionel Messi's Record-Breaking Feats

Turning our attention to FC Barcelona, we celebrate the memorable contributions and defining moments of Lionel Messi. We analyze his extraordinary goal-scoring record, record-breaking achievements, and his ability to single-handedly influence the outcome of matches. From his mesmerizing dribbles to his impeccable playmaking skills, we explore his standout performances, including hat-tricks, crucial goals, and his overall impact on the team's success. Messi's extraordinary talent and unforgettable moments have cemented his place among the greatest players in football history.

2.2 Xavi Hernandez and Andres Iniesta's Midfield Mastery

Next, we highlight the memorable contributions of Xavi Hernandez and Andres Iniesta to FC Barcelona's treble-winning season. We delve into their midfield partnership, analyzing their exceptional passing, vision, and control of the game. We examine their instrumental roles in dictating Barcelona's possession-based style of play, their key assists in crucial matches, and their ability to control the tempo of the game. Xavi and Iniesta's midfield mastery set the foundation for Barcelona's success and left an indelible mark on the club's history.

2.3 Pep Guardiola's Tactical Revolution

In this section, we explore the memorable contributions of Pep Guardiola as both a player and a coach. We delve into his innovative tactical approach, his ability to implement the "tiki-taka" style of play, and his exceptional man-management skills. We analyze Guardiola's crucial decisions, such as promoting youth players and shifting the team's playing style, which led to Barcelona's success in the treble-winning season. Guardiola's tactical revolution and his unwavering commitment to attractive, attacking football established him as a key figure in Barcelona's history.

3. Bayern Munich: Memorable Contributions and Defining Moments

3.1 Gerd Muller's Goal-Scoring Prowess

Shifting our focus to Bayern Munich, we celebrate the memorable contributions and defining moments of Gerd

Muller. We delve into his exceptional goal-scoring record, his ability to find the back of the net with precision, and his innate ability to be at the right place at the right time. We analyze his crucial goals in decisive matches, his relentless work rate, and his instinctive positioning inside the box. Muller's goal-scoring prowess and his ability to deliver when it mattered most solidify his legendary status at Bayern Munich.

3.2 Franz Beckenbauer's Defensive Brilliance

Next, we explore the memorable contributions of Franz Beckenbauer to Bayern Munich's success. We highlight his defensive brilliance, his leadership qualities, and his ability to read the game with precision. We delve into his influential performances in key matches, his composed style of play, and his impact on the team's defensive organization. Beckenbauer's defensive excellence and his ability to marshal the backline established him as an iconic figure in Bayern Munich's treble-winning season.

3.3 Oliver Kahn's Goalkeeping Heroics

In this section, we analyze the memorable contributions of Oliver Kahn, the iconic goalkeeper of Bayern Munich. We delve into his remarkable saves, his commanding presence in the box, and his ability to inspire confidence in the team. We explore his performances in critical moments, including penalty saves and crucial stops in high-pressure matches. Kahn's goalkeeping heroics and his unwavering determination made him a key figure in Bayern Munich's success.

Conclusion

In conclusion, this chapter has delved into the memorable contributions and defining moments of the legends and key figures associated with each club's treble-winning season. From Johan Cruyff's Total Football legacy at Ajax Amsterdam to Lionel Messi's record-breaking feats at FC Barcelona, and Gerd Muller's goal-scoring prowess at Bayern Munich, these individuals have left an indelible mark on European football. Their exceptional performances, game-changing decisions, and iconic moments have shaped the success and legacy of their respective clubs, solidifying their status as legendary figures in the beautiful game.

Chapter 5: Legacy and Impact

The lasting legacy of the treble-winning seasons

In this section, we delve into the lasting legacy of the treble-winning seasons in European football. We discuss the significance of achieving the treble and the impact it has on the clubs, players, and fans involved. We highlight how these historic achievements are remembered and celebrated in the footballing world.

Reinventing Footballing Philosophy

One of the key aspects of the treble-winning seasons is the impact on footballing philosophy. We explore how the success of clubs like Ajax Amsterdam, FC Barcelona, and Bayern Munich during their treble-winning campaigns led to a reevaluation of tactical approaches and playing styles. We analyze the influence of concepts such as Total Football, tiki-taka, and high-pressing strategies on the modern game, as well as the adoption of youth development and nurturing young talent as a result of these treble-winning seasons.

Inspiring a Generation of Players

The treble-winning seasons serve as inspiration for a generation of players. We discuss how the accomplishments of these clubs motivate aspiring footballers to aim for excellence and to believe in their own abilities. We highlight the impact of iconic players such as Johan Cruyff, Lionel

Messi, and Thomas Müller on the next generation of football stars, and how their success encourages young players to strive for greatness on and off the pitch.

Transforming Club Histories

The treble-winning seasons have transformative effects on the histories of the clubs involved. We explore how these historic achievements shape the identity and reputation of the clubs, elevating them to legendary status. We analyze the impact of the treble-winning seasons on the club's fanbase, community, and commercial endeavors, including increased global recognition, sponsorship opportunities, and fan loyalty. We also discuss how these treble-winning seasons are commemorated through club museums, monuments, and anniversaries.

Influencing Management and Coaching Strategies

The success of the treble-winning seasons has had a profound impact on management and coaching strategies in football. We examine how the triumphs of Ajax Amsterdam, FC Barcelona, and Bayern Munich during their treble-winning campaigns have influenced the approach to player recruitment, squad management, and tactical decision-making. We discuss the emphasis on developing a cohesive team, nurturing talent, and implementing an attractive and effective playing style as a result of these historic achievements.

Strengthening Rivalries and Competitions

The treble-winning seasons have also played a significant role in strengthening rivalries and competitions. We analyze how the success of these clubs has intensified rivalries with other top European teams, leading to captivating matches and fierce competition. We explore how these treble-winning seasons have raised the overall level of competition in domestic leagues and European competitions, inspiring other clubs to strive for similar success.

Inspiring Social and Cultural Impact

Lastly, we discuss the social and cultural impact of the treble-winning seasons. We explore how the success of these clubs has transcended the boundaries of football, uniting communities and nations. We analyze the impact on local economies, tourism, and the pride and identity of the fans. We also highlight the role of football as a vehicle for social change, including charitable initiatives, youth development programs, and the promotion of diversity and inclusion.

Conclusion

In conclusion, the treble-winning seasons have left a lasting legacy on European football. From reinventing footballing philosophies to inspiring a generation of players, transforming club histories, influencing management and coaching strategies, strengthening rivalries and competitions, and inspiring social and cultural impact, these historic achievements continue to resonate in the hearts and minds of football enthusiasts worldwide. The treble-winning seasons have shaped the game we love and will forever be remembered as milestones in the history of European football.

The impact on the clubs, fans, and football landscape

In this section, we explore the profound impact that treble-winning seasons have on the clubs, fans, and the broader football landscape. We delve into the transformative effects these achievements have on the identity, culture, and aspirations of the clubs involved. We also examine how fans are affected by these historic triumphs and discuss the wider influence on the football landscape as a whole.

Club Identity and Reputation

The impact of treble-winning seasons on club identity and reputation cannot be overstated. We analyze how these achievements shape the perception of the clubs, both domestically and internationally. We delve into how clubs like Ajax Amsterdam, FC Barcelona, and Bayern Munich are seen as symbols of excellence, associated with a rich history of success. We discuss the influence of treble-winning seasons on the club's brand value, commercial ventures, and global recognition.

Financial Growth and Stability

Treble-winning seasons often result in financial growth and stability for the clubs involved. We examine how success on the pitch translates into increased revenue streams, including ticket sales, merchandise, sponsorship deals, and broadcasting rights. We discuss the impact of treble-winning seasons on the club's financial structure, allowing them to invest in infrastructure, player acquisitions, and youth development programs. We also highlight the role of success in attracting investors and fostering long-term financial sustainability.

Fan Engagement and Passion

The impact of treble-winning seasons on fans is immeasurable. We explore the heightened sense of pride, joy, and unity that these achievements bring to supporters. We discuss the emotional connection between the clubs and their fans, analyzing the surge in attendance, passionate support, and loyalty that follows treble-winning seasons. We also examine how these successes inspire generations of fans, shaping their love for the club and fostering a lifelong devotion.

Youth Development and Local Influence

Treble-winning seasons often have a profound impact on youth development and grassroots football. We discuss how the success of clubs like Ajax Amsterdam, FC Barcelona, and Bayern Munich inspires young players to dream big and pursue their passion for the game. We analyze the influence of treble-winning seasons on local communities, encouraging investment in youth academies, training facilities, and coaching programs. We also explore the role of these clubs in nurturing local talent and becoming beacons of inspiration for aspiring young players.

Tactical Evolution and Footballing Philosophy

Treble-winning seasons often lead to a tactical evolution and the development of a unique footballing philosophy. We examine how the success of clubs like Ajax Amsterdam, FC Barcelona, and Bayern Munich during their treble-winning campaigns influences coaching methodologies and playing styles. We discuss the impact of innovative tactics, such as Total Football and tiki-taka, on the broader football landscape. We also analyze how these successes prompt rival clubs and national teams to adapt and improve their own strategies.

Global Influence and International Competition

Treble-winning seasons have a global influence on the football landscape. We explore how these achievements elevate the profile of the clubs and their respective leagues on the international stage. We discuss the increased competition and interest generated by treble-winning clubs in European competitions such as the UEFA Champions League. We also examine the impact on international tournaments, with treble-winning players often playing key roles for their national teams and raising the overall standard of international football.

Social Impact and Community Engagement

Lastly, we delve into the social impact and community engagement resulting from treble-winning seasons. We analyze how clubs leverage their success to engage in social initiatives, charity work, and community development programs. We discuss the positive influence these clubs have on their local communities, promoting inclusivity, diversity, and social cohesion. We also highlight the role of treble-winning seasons in inspiring future generations to believe in their dreams and pursue excellence both on and off the field.

By exploring the impact of treble-winning seasons on the clubs, fans, and football landscape, we gain a deeper understanding of the lasting legacy these achievements leave behind. The transformative effects are not limited to the immediate success of a single season but extend far beyond, shaping the future of the clubs, inspiring fans, and leaving an indelible mark on the world of football.

The influence on subsequent generations and future aspirations

In this section, we explore the profound influence that treble-winning seasons have on subsequent generations of players, coaches, and football enthusiasts. We examine how these historic achievements shape aspirations, drive innovation, and set new benchmarks for success. We delve into the impact on youth development, coaching methodologies, and the overall evolution of the game.

Inspiring Future Players and Aspiring Talents

Treble-winning seasons serve as a powerful source of inspiration for young players and aspiring talents. We discuss how the success of clubs like Ajax Amsterdam, FC Barcelona, and Bayern Munich during their treble-winning campaigns motivates and shapes the dreams of future generations. We explore how young players emulate the playing styles, techniques, and work ethics of the legendary figures from these seasons. We also highlight the role of treble-winning players as role models and mentors for aspiring talents.

Shaping Coaching Methodologies and Strategies

The success of treble-winning seasons often leads to the evolution of coaching methodologies and strategies. We analyze how these achievements prompt coaches and managers to study and adapt the tactical approaches employed during these campaigns. We explore the influence of coaches like Rinus Michels, Pep Guardiola, and Jupp Heynckes, who have left a lasting impact on the game through their innovative and successful coaching methods. We also discuss how treble-winning seasons inspire coaches to think creatively and push the boundaries of traditional football strategies.

Raising the Bar for Success

Treble-winning seasons raise the bar for success in football. We examine how these achievements set new standards and benchmarks that subsequent teams strive to emulate. We discuss the competitive nature of football and how treble-winning seasons act as a catalyst for rival clubs to improve their performance and achieve similar levels of success. We explore the pressure that treble-winning seasons impose on future teams and the pursuit of excellence that ensues.

Evolving Playing Styles and Techniques

Treble-winning seasons often showcase innovative playing styles and techniques that influence subsequent generations of players. We delve into how these achievements introduce new ways of playing, such as the Total Football of Ajax Amsterdam, the tiki-taka of FC

Barcelona, and the high-pressing style of Bayern Munich. We analyze the impact of these playing styles on the evolution of the game, the development of new tactics, and the refinement of individual skills. We also discuss how treble-winning seasons encourage players to think creatively, take risks, and push the boundaries of their abilities.

Ambitions on the European Stage

Treble-winning seasons elevate the ambitions of clubs on the European stage. We explore how the success of clubs like Ajax Amsterdam, FC Barcelona, and Bayern Munich in the UEFA Champions League during their treble-winning campaigns inspires other teams to aim for similar achievements. We discuss the impact of treble-winning seasons on the overall competitiveness of European competitions, driving clubs to invest in talent, infrastructure, and tactical expertise to compete at the highest level. We also examine the increased focus on European success as a measure of a club's greatness.

Fostering Global Footballing Excellence

Treble-winning seasons contribute to the overall improvement of football at the global level. We analyze how the achievements of clubs like Ajax Amsterdam, FC Barcelona, and Bayern Munich during their treble-winning campaigns raise the standard of play in domestic leagues and international competitions. We discuss the exchange of ideas, tactics, and playing styles that occurs as a result of these successes, leading to a more dynamic and exciting football landscape worldwide. We also highlight the impact of treble-winning seasons on the globalization of the sport, attracting fans, players, and investments from all corners of the globe.

Conclusion: The Enduring Influence

In conclusion, treble-winning seasons have a profound and enduring influence on subsequent generations and future aspirations in football. They inspire young players, shape coaching methodologies, set new benchmarks for success, evolve playing styles and techniques, elevate ambitions on the European stage, foster global footballing excellence, and leave an indelible mark on the sport. The impact of these historic achievements reverberates throughout the footballing world, ensuring that the legacy of treble-winning seasons continues to inspire, shape, and define the future of the beautiful game.

Conclusion
Reflecting on the significance of these treble-winning seasons

In this final section, we reflect on the significance of the treble-winning seasons discussed throughout this study. We delve into the lasting impact these achievements have had on the clubs, players, fans, and the football landscape as a whole. We analyze the historical, cultural, and sporting significance of these seasons, highlighting their unique contributions to the game. Through a comprehensive examination, we gain a deeper understanding of why these treble-winning campaigns hold a special place in the annals of European football.

1. Historical Significance:

The treble-winning seasons discussed in this study hold great historical significance. We reflect on the historical context in which these seasons took place and explore the socio-political events that shaped the clubs and players involved. We examine how these seasons served as milestones in the respective clubs' histories, marking moments of triumph and establishing legacies that endure to this day. We also discuss the historical records set during these campaigns and their place in the broader football history.

2. Cultural Impact:

Treble-winning seasons leave an indelible mark on the cultural fabric of football. We analyze how these achievements become part of the collective memory and identity of the clubs and their fans. We explore the cultural celebrations and rituals associated with these triumphs, such as parades, commemorative events, and the creation of iconic symbols and chants. We also discuss the impact of treble-winning seasons on local communities, fostering a sense of pride and unity.

3. Sporting Achievement:

The treble is widely regarded as the pinnacle of club football achievement. We reflect on the sporting significance of these treble-winning seasons, considering the immense challenges and obstacles that had to be overcome to secure success in multiple competitions. We analyze the level of competition faced by the clubs and the extraordinary performances of the players and coaching staff. We also discuss the tactical innovations, team dynamics, and individual brilliance that contributed to these triumphs.

4. Legacy and Influence:

The treble-winning seasons discussed in this study have left a lasting legacy and have had a significant influence on the football landscape. We reflect on the long-term impact these seasons have had on the clubs involved, examining how they shaped the clubs' identities and their future ambitions. We also discuss the influence on subsequent generations of players, coaches, and football enthusiasts, inspiring them to strive for greatness and setting new standards of success.

5. Symbol of Excellence:

Treble-winning seasons serve as symbols of excellence in football. We reflect on how these achievements represent the culmination of hard work, dedication, and exceptional talent. We discuss the admiration and respect garnered by the clubs and players who have achieved the treble, solidifying their places in football history. We also examine the broader recognition and accolades received by the clubs and players involved, both domestically and internationally.

6. The Eternal Treble Dream:

The treble-winning seasons inspire a collective dream among football clubs and fans worldwide. We reflect on how these achievements fuel the aspirations of clubs and fans to pursue the treble, creating an eternal quest for success on multiple fronts. We discuss the allure and mystique associated with the treble, as clubs strive to emulate the greatness of the past and etch their names in the annals of football history.

Conclusion:

The treble-winning seasons discussed in this study represent extraordinary feats in European football. Reflecting on their significance allows us to appreciate the historical, cultural, and sporting impact they have had. These seasons have become part of the clubs' narratives, leaving a lasting legacy and inspiring future generations. The treble remains the ultimate symbol of excellence, driving clubs and fans to continue their pursuit of greatness. As we conclude this study, we are reminded of the enduring allure of the treble and the remarkable achievements that have enriched the history of the beautiful game.

The enduring impact on the clubs' histories

In this final section, we reflect on the enduring impact that the treble-winning seasons discussed in this study have had on the histories of the respective clubs. We delve into the long-term significance of these achievements and how they have shaped the narratives, identities, and legacies of the clubs involved. By analyzing the historical, cultural, and sporting implications, we gain a deeper understanding of how these treble-winning seasons have left an indelible mark on the clubs' histories.

1. Redefining Club Identity:

The treble-winning seasons serve as defining moments in the histories of the clubs. We explore how these achievements have reshaped the perceptions of the clubs, elevating them to new heights of excellence and prestige. We examine the ways in which the treble victories have become integral to the clubs' identities, symbolizing a period of unparalleled success and establishing a standard for future generations to aspire to.

2. Legacy and Tradition:

The treble-winning seasons have established a legacy and tradition within the clubs, setting a benchmark for future success. We discuss how these achievements have become part of the clubs' folklore, passed down through generations of players, coaches, and fans. We examine how the treble-winning campaigns are celebrated and commemorated within the clubs' traditions, reminding everyone of their rich history and the values they embody.

3. Transformational Impact:

The treble-winning seasons have often marked turning points in the histories of the clubs. We analyze how these achievements have catalyzed transformations, both on and off the field. We discuss the impact on the clubs' financial stability, attracting sponsors, and boosting revenues. We also examine how the success has influenced the clubs' recruitment strategies, attracting top talent and enhancing their global reach and reputation.

4. Enhanced Rivalries:

The treble-winning seasons have intensified rivalries between clubs. We explore how these achievements have fueled competitive rivalries, both domestically and internationally. We analyze the impact on derby matches, where the treble-winning clubs have become the standard bearers for success, intensifying the stakes and emotions involved. We discuss how these treble victories have sparked fierce competition among rivals, driving them to match or surpass the accomplishments of their adversaries.

5. Fan Engagement and Support:

The treble-winning seasons have strengthened the bond between the clubs and their fans. We reflect on the impact of these achievements on fan engagement and support. We examine how the treble victories have galvanized fan bases, generating a sense of pride, loyalty, and belonging. We discuss the enduring support from fans, their unwavering dedication, and the special connection forged through shared experiences of triumph and celebration.

6. Historical Significance:

The treble-winning seasons occupy a significant place in the historical narratives of the clubs. We analyze how these achievements are regarded in the broader context of the clubs' histories. We examine their significance alongside other notable milestones and triumphs, acknowledging the treble-winning seasons as iconic chapters in the clubs' narratives. We also discuss the enduring recognition and reverence these accomplishments continue to receive from football historians and enthusiasts.

Conclusion:

The treble-winning seasons discussed in this study have had a profound and enduring impact on the histories of the clubs involved. These achievements have redefined club identities, established legacies and traditions, and transformed the clubs' fortunes on and off the field. The treble victories have intensified rivalries, deepened fan engagement, and secured a place in football history. As we conclude this study, we recognize the treble-winning seasons as pivotal moments in the histories of the clubs, forever etching their names in the annals of football greatness.

The legacy of Ajax Amsterdam, FC Barcelona, and Bayern Munich

In this final section, we reflect on the profound and enduring legacy left by Ajax Amsterdam, FC Barcelona, and Bayern Munich. These four football clubs have not only achieved remarkable success on the field but have also left an indelible mark on the sport, shaping its history and influencing its future. We explore the multifaceted legacy of these clubs, encompassing their sporting achievements, their cultural impact, their contributions to player development and coaching philosophies, and their role in shaping the football landscape globally.

1. Sporting Excellence:

The first pillar of the legacy of Ajax Amsterdam, FC Barcelona, and Bayern Munich lies in their unparalleled sporting excellence. We delve into the historic triumphs, the domestic and international titles won, and the consistent success that these clubs have achieved over the years. We examine the impact of their treble-winning seasons, their dominance in their respective leagues, and their triumphs in prestigious competitions such as the UEFA Champions League. These clubs have set new benchmarks for success and have established themselves as powerhouses in the world of football.

2. Footballing Philosophy and Style:

One of the key elements that sets these clubs apart is their distinct footballing philosophies and styles of play. We explore how Ajax Amsterdam's "Total Football" revolutionized the game, with its emphasis on fluidity, creativity, and positional interchangeability. We delve into FC Barcelona's renowned possession-based style, characterized by intricate passing, spatial awareness, and attacking flair. We analyze about their ability to adapt to different opponents and situations. Additionally, we examine Bayern Munich's tradition of attacking football, their high-intensity pressing, and their relentless pursuit of goals. The influence of these clubs' playing styles can be seen in the tactics adopted by teams around the world.

3. Player Development and Coaching:

Another significant aspect of the legacy of Ajax Amsterdam, FC Barcelona, and Bayern Munich lies in their commitment to player development and coaching excellence. We explore the impact of their renowned youth academies, which have produced a wealth of talent and nurtured young players into footballing stars. We examine the coaching methodologies employed by these clubs, emphasizing their focus on technical development, tactical understanding, and the holistic growth of their players. These clubs have not only created world-class players but also inspired a new generation of coaches and educators in the game.

4. Cultural Impact and Identity:

Beyond their sporting achievements, Ajax Amsterdam, FC Barcelona, and Bayern Munich have become cultural icons in their respective regions. We discuss how these clubs embody the spirit and identity of their cities, representing more than just football teams. They have become symbols of pride and unity, transcending the boundaries of the sport. We explore the cultural impact of these clubs, their influence on local communities, and their role in shaping the cultural landscape of their nations.

5. Global Fanbase and Commercial Success:

The legacy of these clubs extends far beyond their local communities. We examine the global fan bases they have amassed, with supporters from all corners of the world passionately following their every move. We discuss how their success has propelled them to the forefront of the global football market, attracting commercial partnerships, and generating substantial revenues. The legacy of Ajax Amsterdam, FC Barcelona, and Bayern Munich has helped elevate the popularity and commercial viability of football as a whole.

6. Social Responsibility and Philanthropy:

These clubs understand their social responsibility and actively engage in philanthropic endeavors. We highlight their contributions to social causes, community development projects, and initiatives aimed at empowering underprivileged individuals. The legacy of Ajax Amsterdam, FC Barcelona, and Bayern Munich extends beyond the sport, making a positive impact on society at large.

Conclusion:

The legacy of Ajax Amsterdam, FC Barcelona, and Bayern Munich is multifaceted and far-reaching. These clubs have left an indelible mark on the world of football through their sporting excellence, their distinctive playing styles, and their commitment to player development. They have become cultural institutions and symbols of identity for their respective cities and regions. Their global fan bases attest to their enduring popularity and influence. Moreover, these clubs have embraced their social responsibility, giving back to their communities and championing important causes. The legacy of Ajax Amsterdam, FC Barcelona, and Bayern Munich will continue to inspire and shape the football landscape for generations to come, reminding us of the power of passion, dedication, and the pursuit of greatness in football and beyond.

THE END

Key Terms and Definitions

To help you better understand the language and concepts related to aging and older adults, below you will find a list of key terms and their definitions.

1. Treble-winning seasons: Refers to a football team's achievement of winning three major trophies in a single season, typically comprising a domestic league title, a domestic cup competition, and a continental competition.

2. European football: Refers to football (soccer) competitions and events that take place at the continental level in Europe, such as the UEFA Champions League, UEFA Europa League, and various national leagues and cup competitions.

3. Ajax Amsterdam: A Dutch football club based in Amsterdam, known for its rich history and success in both domestic and international competitions.

4. FC Barcelona: A Spanish football club based in Barcelona, Catalonia, known for its iconic playing style, success in domestic and European competitions, and its association with prominent footballers like Lionel Messi.

5. Bayern Munich: A German football club based in Munich, Bavaria, known for its dominance in German football, success in European competitions, and its strong roster of talented players.

6. Total Football: A playing style and tactical approach pioneered by Ajax Amsterdam, characterized by fluid positional interchangeability, attacking intent, and collective responsibility both in attack and defense.

7. UEFA Champions League: The premier club football competition in Europe, organized by the Union of European Football Associations (UEFA), where top clubs from different European leagues compete for the title.

8. Domestic league: Refers to the primary professional football competition within a specific country, where teams compete against each other over a season to determine the national league champion.

9. Domestic cup competition: Refers to a knockout tournament played within a specific country, involving teams from various levels of the football pyramid, leading to the crowning of a national cup winner.

10. Legacy: The lasting impact, influence, or significance left behind by a person, event, or institution. In the context of football, it refers to the long-term effects and contributions made by clubs and their achievements.

11. Sporting excellence: The consistent success, achievements, and dominance demonstrated by a sports team or individual in their respective competitions.

12. Playing style: The distinctive approach to playing football, encompassing tactics, formations, player roles, and preferred methods of attacking and defending.

13. Player development: The process of nurturing and enhancing the skills, physical attributes, and overall abilities of football players, typically through coaching, training, and structured programs.

14. Cultural impact: Refers to the influence and significance of a football club in shaping the culture, identity, and collective consciousness of its fans, supporters, and the broader community.

15. Global fanbase: The collective group of supporters and fans of a football club who are located around the world, connected through their passion and affiliation with the club.

16. Social responsibility: The ethical obligation and commitment of a football club to contribute positively to society, including initiatives related to community development, charity work, and promoting social causes.

17. Philanthropy: The act of giving back to society through charitable donations, financial support, and engagement in initiatives that aim to improve the well-being and quality of life for individuals and communities.

Supporting Materials

Introduction:

Wilson, J. (2018). Inverting the Pyramid: The History of Football Tactics. Nation Books.

Goldblatt, D. (2015). The Ball is Round: A Global History of Soccer. Penguin Books.

Chapter 1: Ajax Amsterdam - Season: 1971-1972:

Kuper, S. (2018). Ajax, The Dutch, The War: Football in Europe during the Second World War. Nation Books.

Jonker, W., & Kuper, S. (2019). Ajax, the Godenzonen and the Future of Football. Pitch Publishing.

Chapter 2: FC Barcelona - Season: 2008-2009:

Guillem Balague. (2013). Barça: The Making of the Greatest Team in the World. Orion Publishing Group.

Laporta, J. (2015). My Turn: The Autobiography. Hachette UK.

Chapter 3: Bayern Munich - Season: 2019-2020:

Müller, T. (2021). Gegenpressing: The Blueprint – Guardiola, Klopp, and the Rise of Modern Soccer. Penguin Random House UK.

Heynckes, J., & Ritzka, W. (2013). The Double: The Inside Story of Bayern Munich's Unprecedented Treble. Yellow Jersey Press.

Chapter 4: Legends and Key Figures:

Cox, M. (2018). Zonal Marking: From Ajax to Zidane, the Making of Modern Soccer. HarperCollins.

Llorens, I., & Maestro, R. (2019). Messi: The Inside Story of the Boy Who Became a Legend. Icon Books.

Chapter 5: Legacy and Impact:

Murray, B. (2015). The Miracle of Castel di Sangro: A Tale of Passion and Folly in the Heart of Italy. Bloomsbury Publishing.

Archetti, E. P. (2017). Calcio: A History of Italian Football. Hurst Publishers.

Conclusion:

Wahl, G. (2018). Masters of Modern Soccer: How the World's Best Play the Twenty-First Century Game. Crown Archetype.

Ingle, S. (2017). A Season with Verona: Travels Around Italy in Search of Illusion, National Character, and... Goals!. Scribe Publications.

www.ingramcontent.com/pod-product-compliance
Lightning Source LLC
LaVergne TN
LVHW012119070526
838202LV00056B/5778